DAVID PAUL WERNER

THE TREES SHALL SING!

Hymn Accompaniments for Organ

45 organ-settings of 32 chorale and hymn tunes
to lead, enrich and uplift congregational singing

Christian Arts Foundation

Cover design © by David Paul Werner
Cover photo © by Andreas Präfcke, use by permission
Rückpositiv, Christuskirche, Stuttgart (Walcker, 1957)
Title rendered from I Chronicles 16:33, Psalm 96:12, Isaiah 44:23

Appreciation and gratitude to:
Kathryn Ann Hill and Michael James Hill for their editorial assistance
hymnary.org for their comprehensive hymn database and resources

Published by Christian Arts Foundation, www.caf.org.hk
Country of origin shown on last page.

ISBN 978-988-18820-6-6

Table of Contents

Alphabetical index by commonly associated texts

Index by common liturgical associations

Performance notes

Usage: These hymn settings are primarily intended to support congregational singing. They are styled to transition smoothly from harmonizations given in widely used hymnals. Meters, keys and tune variants have been chosen to comply with a broad sampling of these hymnals. These settings can also serve as mini-études for teaching, or, with adjustments to registration and tempo, as preludes, postludes and interludes. Settings in 4 or 5 parts offer ready opportunities for instrumentalists to join, and some settings can be sung in parts.

Registration: Suggestions here are based on a prototypical 2-manual church organ (exemplified below). They serve as liberal guides to timbre, balance and overarching effect. The fundamental manuals registration to lead congregational singing is a diapason-based ensemble of 8 ft. and 4 ft. flue pipes with discretionary upperwork (Foundations 8' 4') and open expression shutters. This basic registration is refined for each organ, for each hymn, to be tonally sympathetic to the hymn text and scaled to the size of the congregation. Pedal registrations should optimize tonal blend, clarity of line and balanced bass.

Notation conventions:
- Phrasing is generally not indicated because it may vary according to different texts applied to the same tune.
- Common notes passing from one voice to another are often not shown as tied, but in legato playing are to be tied unless a rearticulation (/) is indicated, or if it would result in a tie to a descending melodic line on the same manual.
- Dynamics from *pp* to *f* indicate relative position of expression shutters, from fully closed to fully open.
- Wedges ($\prec$ $\succ$) or text *cresc.* and *dim.* indicate gradual opening and closing of expression shutters.
- $+$Reg. and $-$Reg. means to add and remove registers (*i.e.*, stops), respectively.
- *ff* indicates full or relatively full organ with expression shutters open.
- Divisional abbreviations are G or Gt. for Great (primary manual), S or Sw. for Swell (subordinate manual), and Ped. for Pedal.
- GS on manual staves means play on Great with Swell coupled.
- G, S or GS on the pedal staff indicates which manuals are coupled to the pedal.
- Solo on the pedal staff means no manual-to-pedal couplers are engaged.

D. P. W.

First Presbyterian Church, Wonju, Korea Beckerath, 2006			St. Andrew Lutheran Church, Beaverton OR, USA Fritts, 1993		
Hauptwerk	Schwellwerk	Pedal	Man. I	Man. II	Pedal
8' Principal	8' Rohrflöte	16' Subbaß	16' Quintadena	8' Rohrflöte	16' Subbaß
8' Spielflöte	8' Salicional	8' Octavbaß	8' Principal	8' Gemshorn	8' Principal
4' Oktave	4' Hohlflöte	8' Offenflöte	8' Rohrflöte	4' Spitzgedackt	8' Gedackt
4' Spitzflöte	II Sesquialtera	4' Choralbaß	4' Octav	2' Waldflöte	4' Octav
$2^2/_3$' Quinte	2' Principal	IV Rauschpfeife	$2^2/_3$' Nasat (half)	$1^1/_3$' Sifflöte	16' Posaune
2' Offenflöte	IV Scharf	16' Fagott	II Cornet (full)	8' Trichterregal	8' Trompet
V Mixtur	8' Hautbois		2' Octav		
8' Trompete			IV Mixtur		
			8' Trompet		

1. Adeste Fideles

Intrada, last stanza, optional brass
"Yea, Lord, we greet Thee"
"Ergo qui natus"

Intrada

Stanza

NOTE: Last four meaures of Intrada can
serve as alternate ending for Stanza.

1a. Adeste Fideles

Brass parts

NOTE: Last four measures of Intrada can
serve as alternate ending for Stanza.

2. All Ehr und Lob

in G and F major

3. Allein Gott in der Höh
in G and F major, and tune variant in F

Gt.: Foundations, clear and light
Sw.: Foundations, with Cromorne or Cornet
Ped.: Foundations (16') 8' 4', Dulzian or Fagott 16'

Gioiosa e danzante

G
S
Ped. solo
"Allein Gott in der Höh"
tune variant
Ped.

4. Antioch

Man.: Founds. full, clear and bright
Ped.: Founds. with Reed 8' or 16'

NOTE: To reduce duration of sung note to a dotted quarter, omit m. 7, and play lowest D and A beginning m. 8 one octave higher than written.

5. Chesterfield (Richmond)

in canon at the fourth

Gt.: Foundations 8' 4'
Sw.: Foundations 8' 4' with Oboe or Nazard
Ped.: Bourdons 16' 8', Principal 8'

6. Coronation

Four stanzas with key change

Gt.: Foundations 8' 4'
Sw.: Foundations full
Ped.: Foundations 16' 8' 4'

4

9

15
+ Sw. Reeds
Man.
20
25
30
+ Gt. 2' mp più legato
Man.
36
mf
f mf

41
allargando

46
Marcato e risoluto
ff
Ped. (G)S

51

56

7. Darwall's 148th

Man.: Foundations 8' 4' 2', Mix., Sw. Oboe
Ped.:   Foundations 16' 8' 4', Reed 8' or 16'

8. Deo Gracias (Agincourt)

in C and D minor

Elaboration of a setting
by E. Power Biggs

Gt.: Full Foundations
Sw.: Full, with Reeds and Cornet
Ped.: Foundations with Reeds

8a. Deo Gracias (Agincourt)

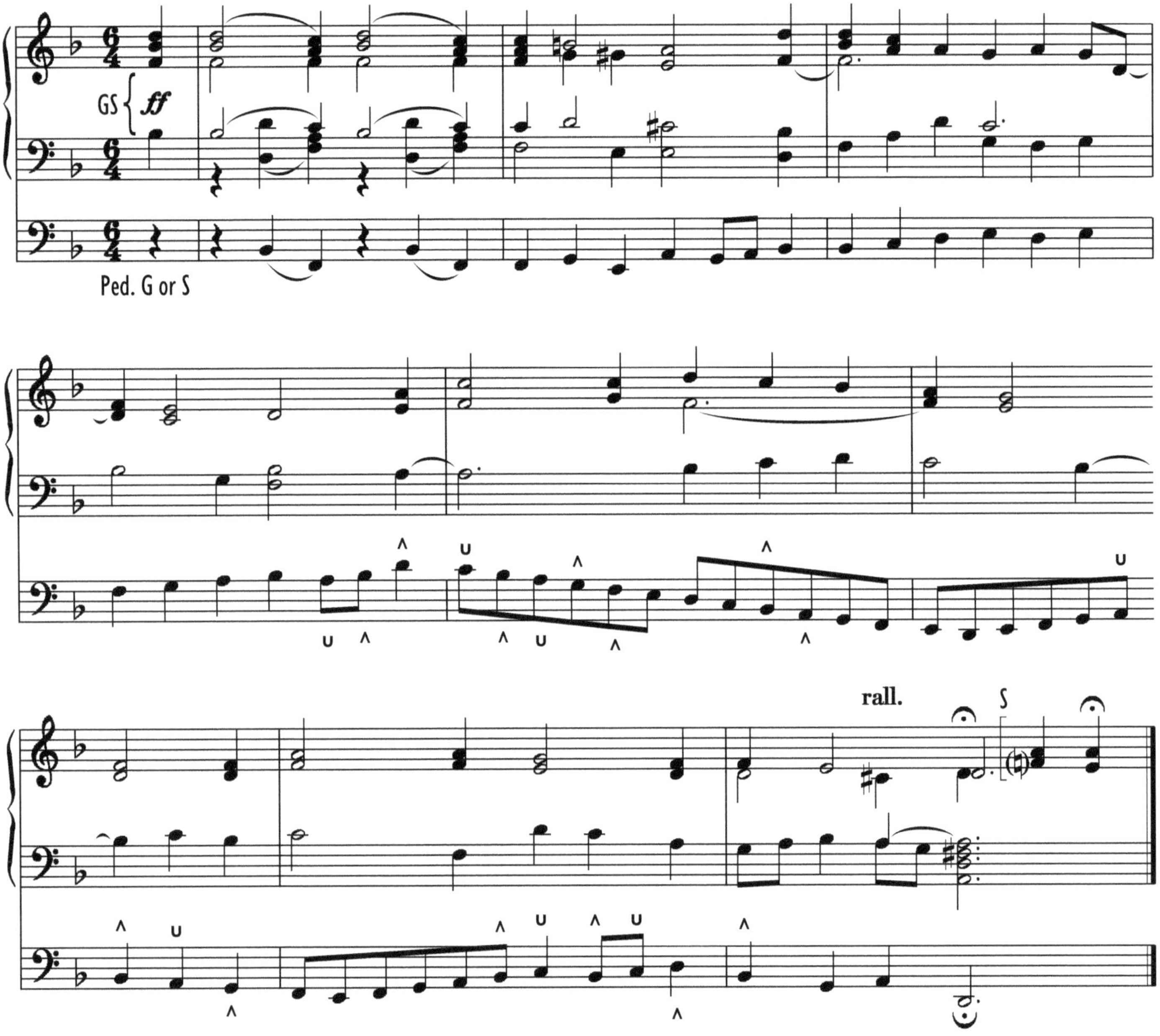

9. Eventide

Key change and last stanza

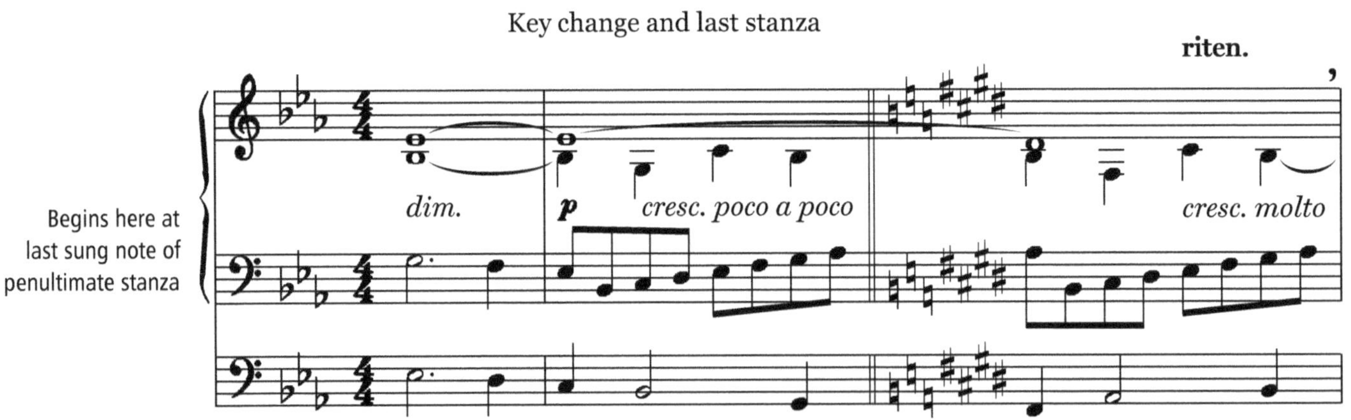

a tempo
ff sostenuto
rall.

10. Freut euch, ihr lieben Christen

Intrada and stanza

Integrated with music from
Prélude Liturgiques XI
by Gaston Litaize

Man.: Foundations 8' 4' 2', Mix., Oboe or Cromorne
Ped.: Foundations 16' 8' 4', Fagott or Dulzian 16'

Stanza
GS
Ped. S

11. Gelobt sei Gott (Vulpius)

Three stanzas

29
34
39
+ Mix., Reed 16' or 8'
Ped. Founds. 16' 8' 4'
No reed to pedal
44
51
riten.

12. Greensleeves

13. Helft mir Gotts Güte preisen

14. Herr Jesu Christ, meins

Ped.

"Herr Jesu Christ, meins" tune variant

15. Herzliebster Jesu in G and F minor

16. Jesu, meines Lebens Leben

Settings for penultimate and last stanzas

"Then, for all that wrought my pardon"
"Nun ich danke dir von Herzen"
18
a tempo un poco più largamente
sia pesante sia luminoso
22
26
30
+ Reg.

17. Lasst uns erfreuen

Key change and last stanza

Elaboration of a setting
by R. Vaughan Williams

NOTE: To play as a 3/2 measure, omit the middle two pedal
notes, C and B-flat, and change whole notes to half notes.

18. Lobe den herren

Prelude (below), key change and last stanza (overleaf)

NOTE: This may be played as a stand-alone prelude
from m. 7, ending on an F major chord after m. 29.

Key change and last stanza overleaf >

19. Melita

"When He shall come with trumpet sound"

Man.: Founds. 8' 4' 2', Mixtures
Ped.: Founds. 16' 8' 4', Trumpet 8'

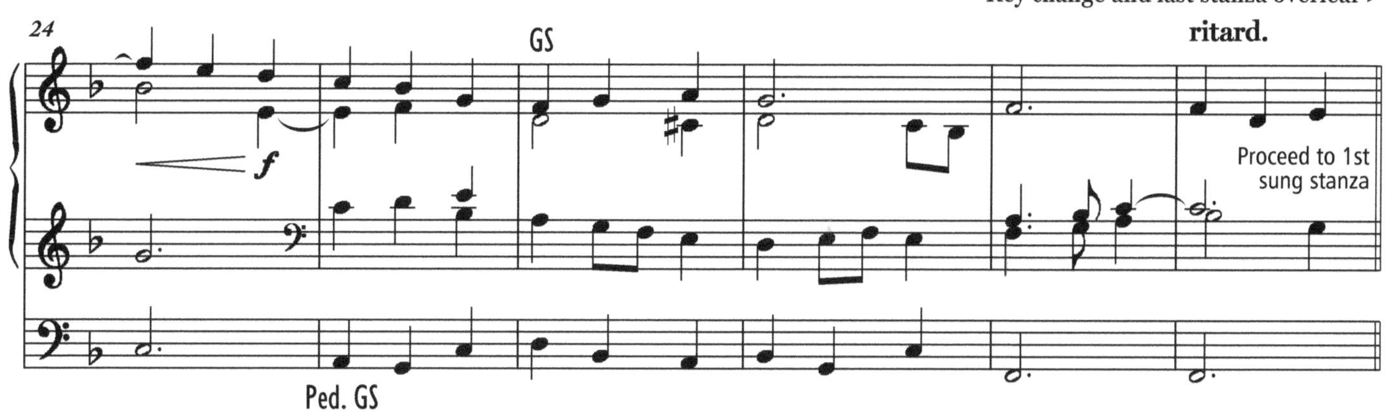

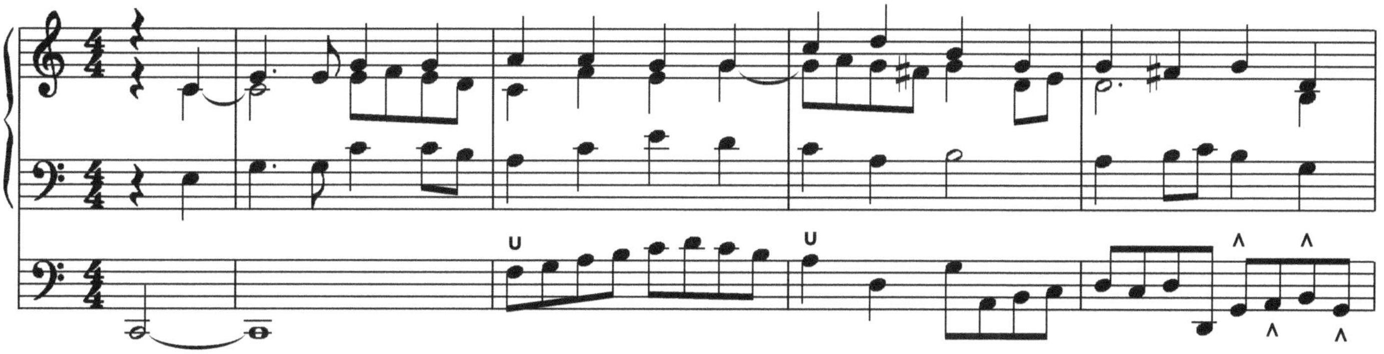

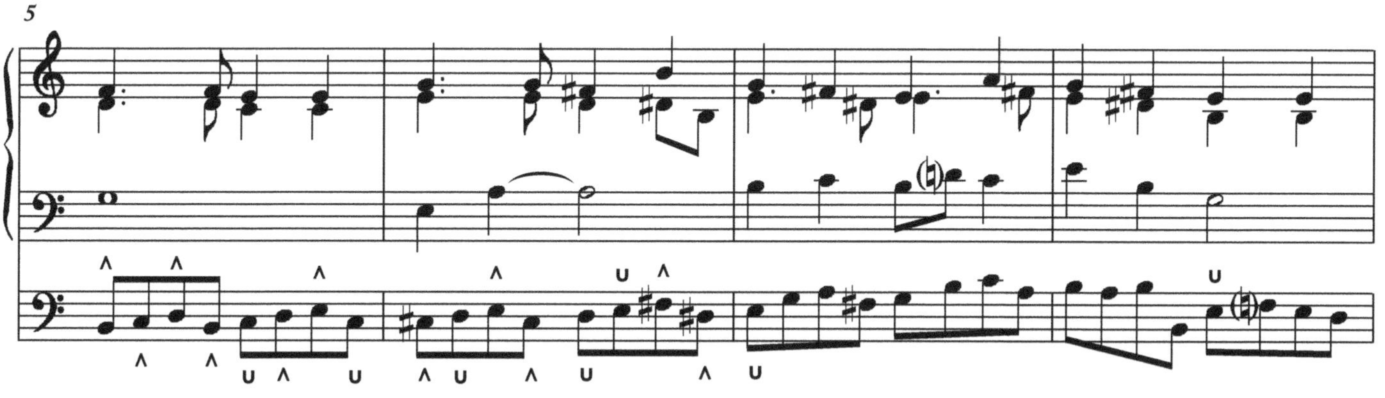

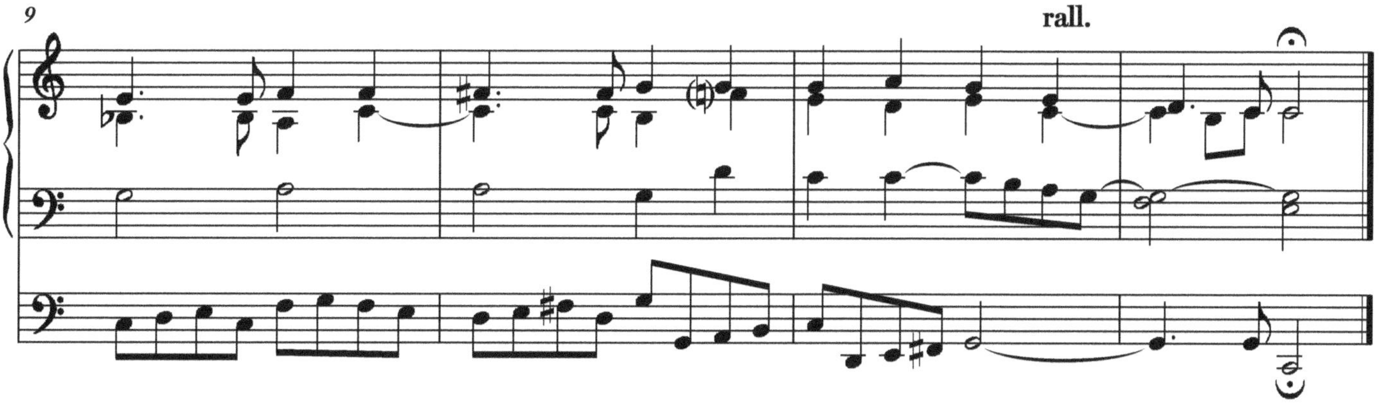

Begins here at last sung note
of penultimate stanza:
30
18a. Lobe den Herren
Key change and last stanza
ritard.
34
a tempo
+ Reg.
Ped.
39
44
49
Edition CAF
~ 36 ~

20. Mendelssohn

21. Noël Nouvelet

in E and F dorian

Gt.: Foundations 8' 4', Cornet or Reed
Sw.: Foundations 8' 4'
Ped.: Foundations 16' 8'

22. Nun danket all
(Gräfenberg)
Ped.

23. Old Hundredth

Intrada and two stanzas

~ 40 ~

Stanza or recessional
20
24
27
più largando
30
l.h.
~ 41 ~

24. O du Liebe meiner Liebe

25. Patmos

Two stanzas

26. Regent Square

Two versions—with pedal, and manuals only

Gt.: Foundations 8' 4' 2'
Sw.: Foundations 8' 4', with Cymbale, Scharf or 19th
Ped.: Foundations 16' 8' (4')

Gt. Foundations 8' 4' 2' (opt. l.h. on Sw. 8' 4', with Cymbale, Scharf or 19th)
legato

27. St. Cross
Ped.

28. St. George's, Windsor
Full Foundations, with Sw. & Ped. Reeds
Vigoroso
GS
Ped. S
rall.
Edition CAF
~ 46 ~

29.
Seelenbräutigam
Versions in irregular
and regular meters
Ped.
3
Ped.
~ 47 ~

30. Slane

Key change and last stanza

31. Tallis' Canon

32. Windham